Original title:
A Symphony of Waves

Copyright © 2025 Creative Arts Management OÜ
All rights reserved.

Author: Elliot Harrison
ISBN HARDBACK: 978-1-80581-617-1
ISBN PAPERBACK: 978-1-80581-144-2
ISBN EBOOK: 978-1-80581-617-1

The Gentle Symphony of Sheltered Bays

In the bay where seagulls squawk,
Crabs dance a silly, sideways walk.
Fishes splash, making tiny waves,
While jellyfish sway like ocean babes.

Turtles glide with a goofy grin,
Chasing bubbles, oh, what a win!
The sun sets, casting fiery rays,
As dolphins join in silly plays.

Drift into the Ocean's Embrace

Float on waves, a rubber duck,
Giggling as we run amok.
A starfish wears my old flip-flop,
While seaweed does a quirky hop.

Mermaids laugh with glittery tails,
Trading secrets in ocean trails.
The tide pulls in with quite a shove,
As sea cucumbers dance in love.

Time's Cadence under the Stars

Night falls, the moon's a giant pie,
The stars are popcorn in the sky.
Crickets chirp a funny tune,
While waves whisper secrets to the moon.

A fish winks with a playful eye,
As laughter echoes, oh my, oh my!
Time trickles like dripping ice cream,
As we drift off in this quirky dream.

Conductor of Celestial Waters

In rubber boots, he waves his hands,
 The fish all dance, do silly bands.
 Seagulls swoop, a feathery choir,
 Flapping wings fuel his wild fire.

With a splash here, a splash there,
 The crabs join in, without a care.
 Octopus plays the dizzy sax,
While shrimp provide the silly tracks.

Tidal Brushstrokes on Sand

The tide rolls in, a goofy clown,
Painting smiles on the shoreline frown.
Seashells giggle, and driftwood grins,
As seaweed curls and does the spins.

Footprints chase like a game of tag,
While dolphins dance, all wag and brag.
The beachball bounces, sandy and bright,
As laughter echoes under the light.

Aural Poetry of the Ocean's Heart

Shells whisper secrets, tales of the deep,
Crashing waves sing spells that leap.
The tide hums notes, a quirky tune,
While starfish groove beneath the moon.

Nautical notes from a jazzed-up whale,
Mermaids giggle, chasing a sail.
Clams snap shut, shy from the show,
But the barnacles cheer, "Let's go, let's go!"

The Caress of Briny Breezes

A breeze waltzes in, tickles your nose,
With salty whispers, it happily goes.
The kites above flap, a vibrant spree,
Laughing at clouds, as wild as can be.

Wind-chimes clank in melodious cheer,
While beachgoers laugh and share a beer.
Sandy toes dance, a raucous delight,
As the sunset giggles, "What a night!"

Serenade of the Shoreline Breeze

Seagulls squawk in a silly choir,
Chasing crumbs tossed by a beach bonfire.
Sandcastles wobbly, with smiles that gleam,
While kids dig holes like it's a big dream.

The tide rolls in, it's a slippery race,
Running from waves, oh, what a fun chase!
Buckets and shovels, the tools of the trade,
Where laughter and splashes are frequently made.

Dance of the Fluid Currents

Bubbles pop like a fizzy drink,
Fish perform in a watery wink.
Seaweed sways like a funky dancer,
With each wave's push, it's a bubbly enhancer.

Surfboards tipping like clumsy boats,
Riders giggling, clutching their coats.
Oh, look! A crab in a whimsical stroll,
With pincers waving like it's on a roll!

Chorus of the Sea Foam

Frothy waves sing with a giggling sound,
Tickling toes as they roll on the ground.
Starfish audition for a splashy role,
Bouncing around, they've got soul!

Paddleboarders wobble, they trip and they sway,
As seagulls drop snacks, oh what a display!
A beach ball soars in a wild, grand arc,
Splashing laughter ignites with a spark.

The Language of Flowing Waters

Rivers chuckle with pebbles in tow,
Whispers of fish that gracefully flow.
Turtles in shades brimming with pride,
They glide through the currents, oh what a ride!

Puddles giggle when kids splish-splash,
Making tiny waves with a joyful crash.
The sun dips low, with a wink and a gleam,
As nighttime dances to the water's gleam.

Reflections of Harmony in Motion

The seagulls dance in silly flight,
Their shadows skip, what a funny sight!
Waves crash in giggles, a watery cheer,
As fish wear hats, oh what a sphere!

Sunshine winks from ocean's face,
As turtles glide with unmatched grace.
Crabs doing bumps on sandy lawns,
The beach party starts before the dawn!

Jellyfish bounce like rubber balls,
Dancing beneath the blue water halls.
An octopus juggles shells with glee,
While sea stars applaud in the sea!

With every splash, there's laughter loud,
Fishes frolic beneath a cloud.
In this concert of bubbly fun,
Ocean's jokes are second to none!

Chord of the Ocean's Breath

Seashells sing in a groundbeat tune,
While seaweed sways beneath the moon.
A clam's a drummer in its own band,
Making rhythms in the soft sand!

Dolphins leap in a joyous spree,
Waves clapping back, let's all agree!
Every splash is a punchline bright,
As turtles laugh through the starry night!

Crabs in tuxedos tap their feet,
Every little pincher's got some beat!
Fishes whisper secrets of delight,
Tickling currents in the pale moonlight!

The ocean hums its funny song,
Where every wave just helps us along.
No need to fret, just sway and glide,
In this watery jest, let's all take a ride!

Sonorous Waves of Tranquil Bliss

Bubbles rise with each giddy burst,
In this ocean fun, we can't help but thirst!
The plankton glow like a disco ball,
While whale's high notes echo through the hall!

Surfers ride the wavy tow,
In brightly colored suits, the star of the show.
A starfish jokes, 'I'm the best on land!'
While seashells giggle at each grain of sand!

Every tide has a tale to tell,
A ship's anchor wishes it could dwell.
With dolphins darting all around,
They're the jokers of this ocean sound!

From fishy pranks to tidal plays,
The underwater crowd loves to amaze.
In every splash, a chuckle awaits,
For the waves sure know how to celebrate!

The Undulating Melody of The Blue

A whale, in deep voice, cracks a joke,
While jellyfish twirl in their silken cloak.
Sea cucumbers roll with delight,
'We can't dance, but we sure look right!'

The sun tickles the sea with a grin,
As waves go swaying, letting fun begin.
Little fish dart, making quick hits,
Around coral castles, they do their skits!

With every wave in a rhythmic churn,
The audience cheers for the twists and turns.
Snapping shrimp create a great sound,
Each little bubble becomes profound!

Underwater laughter echoes profound,
In this cartoon world, there's joy all around.
Come join the fun, let's all be bold,
In the water's embrace, our stories unfold!

A Canvas of Rolling Deep

The ocean paints with foam and glee,
A seagull swoops, oh, what a spree!
Each splash a tickle, each wave a laugh,
As crabs do the cha-cha, on the sand they gaff.

Seaweed dances, a silly waltz,
While dolphins tease with playful faults.
A beach ball bounces, kids all cheer,
Splash fights ensue, full of good-natured jeer.

Shells are hats for the cheeky fish,
They flip and flounder, their only wish.
An octopus juggles with flair so grand,
While starfish giggle, all over the sand.

The sunlight winks, a jester bright,
As surfers crash with joyful might.
The tide rolls in, it's time to play,
In this rolling deep, we laugh away.

The Whispering Dunes at Dusk

The dunes are giggling, soft and sweet,
As tumbleweeds join in with their beat.
Sand castles tumble with a woosh,
While kids yell out, "Hey, watch this swoosh!"

The wind whispers secrets in a sly tone,
As flip-flops dance; they're not alone.
A lizard laughs, a wiggle and dash,
While a coyote joins in with a flash.

Stars peek out, like sprinkles on cake,
While shadows stretch, just for fun's sake.
The moon starts to chuckle, a beacon so bright,
As the dunes get sillier, into the night.

With every sand grain, a ticklish tale,
As distant echoes of laughter prevail.
The whispers carry, sweet and low,
Dunes at dusk, in a merry show.

Tidal Melodies and Celestial Rhythms

Rhythms crash upon the shore,
A melody of giggles, wanting more.
Seashells hum, a silly tune,
Whilst crabs tap dance under the moon.

The tides do tango, swaying about,
Splashing all with a playful shout.
Fish joke with bubbles, blowing with glee,
While starfish snicker at the ruckusy spree.

The lighthouse beams, a quirky eye,
Keeping watch with a wink, oh my!
As surfers glide on laughter's crest,
Each wave an encore, in this jested fest.

Oceanic lullabies, soft and neat,
Filled with fun, a rumbly beat.
In every splash, there's a giggle retained,
In tidal adventures, joy is unchained.

The Silhouette of a Distant Wave

A shadow stretches, tall and wide,
A wave rehearses, no need to hide.
It wobbles and shimmies, things getting funny,
The crowd of folks laughs, oh isn't that sunny!

With every rise, there's a playful jump,
As kids in their floaties give a little thump.
The horizon teases, a dreamy sight,
With splashes of laughter, the evening's delight.

The sun bows low, a cheeky grin,
As waves keep twirling, let the fun begin!
A silhouette dances, swaying so grand,
As everyone claps on the pale, soft sand.

Each wave a story, a twist of fate,
With giggles erupting, we just can't wait.
So let's ride the punchlines, surf the good cheer,
In the silhouette of fun, let's persevere!

The Undulating Chorus

The ocean dances, oh so spry,
With splashes tickling seagulls high.
A fish in a tux, what a sight!
Bows to the dolphin, oh what a night!

The waves clap hands, it's quite absurd,
They cheer for sailors, or is it a bird?
Crabs with top hats, they tap their claws,
Declaring sea parties with a round of applause!

Shells sing softly, their secrets out,
While currents giggle, there's no doubt.
Turtles in shades, strut with flair,
While jellyfish glide, floating in air!

In this salty realm, laughter beams,
Where seaweed jokes flow like wild dreams.
So join the fun, don't be shy,
The ocean's theatre is standing by!

Ballad of the Endless Ocean

The waves roll in with a wobbly glee,
The seagulls laugh, oh what a spree!
Clams tell tales of mariner's gaffes,
While sardines giggle at silly past jazz.

Fish in bow ties twirl their fins,
As the sea horse spins in dizzy grins.
Octopuses serve cocktails from their dens,
Mollusks can't dance, but try now and then!

A ship with a parrot named Chuck
Sails through the blues with a stroke of luck.
He squawks jokes 'till the stars shine bright,
As laughter echoes through the night!

So here's to the sea, a jolly affair,
Where humor flows free, without a care.
Raise your glass, let's toast with cheer,
To the endless ocean, the life we hold dear!

Whispers of the Moonlit Sea

Under moonlight, the waves start to jest,
Crabs play hide and seek, they're the best!
A starfish debates with a wandering tide,
While whispers of laughter in the surf collide.

The flounder, a joker, tells tales so grand,
Of adventures and seaweed made into land.
Whales pull pranks with their watery might,
Creating splashes that dance through the night!

If you listen closely, the seashells hum,
Of mermaids winking, saying, "Here they come!"
With shells on their heads, they shimmy and sway,
The moonlit sea's party makes worries stray!

So sail through the currents, let laughter unfurl,
In this world of dreams, let joy twirl.
For in the ocean's embrace, we unite,
Under stars and waves, oh what a delight!

The Ocean's Embrace: A Lyric Journey

The sea calls out with giggles so bold,
As jellyfish dance in dresses of gold.
Seagulls narrate mismatched love tales,
While crabs crack jokes, sending up sails!

In the ocean's arms, there's no need to fret,
Starfish bake muffins, it's quite the duet!
With sea cucumbers wiggling in cheer,
And dolphins who drum, laugh rings in the air!

A narwhal sings songs about treasure maps,
While the tide sways gently, avoiding mishaps.
With surfboards made of driftwood and dreams,
We ride the waves, laughter bursting at seams!

So hop aboard this sea-faring spree,
Where humor and kindness flow wild and free.
In every splash, in every cheer,
The ocean embraces, and brings us near!

Dreamscapes Above the Rolling Deep

Bubbles dance and giggle, oh what a sight,
A crab in a tuxedo, feeling quite bright.
Seagulls laugh like they own the whole place,
While fish do the cha-cha, it's a lively space.

Waves whisper secrets, in watery tones,
With clams telling jokes on their shiny, cool stones.
Octopus juggling shells just for a thrill,
While the starfish looks on with an absolute chill.

Calls of the Sea's Hidden Choir

A whale hits high notes, quite off the key,
While dolphins join in, as happy as can be.
The seaweed sways like it's lost in the beat,
And the tide keeps the rhythm with its bubbling feet.

Starfish are clappers, shells shake along,
Except for the crab, who is short of a song.
But oh, what a tune from that clam by the shore,
Who suddenly yells, 'I'm an opera star!'

Messages Carried by the Wind and Surf

A bottle rolls in with a jolly good cheer,
Carrying jokes from the ocean so near.
The wind sends whispers, much like a prank,
Sea turtles giggle, giving it thanks.

The waves bring a letter from an otter named Lou,
Saying, 'Join my party, you'll have a great view!'
With krill as the snacks and plankton for drink,
It sounds like a bash, or so I do think!

The Sound of Dreaming Waves

The tide rolls in with a snore and a sigh,
As jellyfish float, they wave me goodbye.
Shells circle around like they're lost in a trance,
While sea cucumbers try their first dance.

In the frothy bubbles, dreams start to swim,
A mermaid is searching for some new bling.
But her treasure map's made of soggy old kelp,
Oh, what a journey! I might need some help!

The Gentle Clamor of the Seaside

The seagulls squawk in perfect tone,
As tourists dance in sand like clowns.
With ice cream cones that melt and moan,
They plop like fish and fall in towns.

A crab in shades walks proud and bold,
While sunbathers bake like giant pies.
Surfboards tumble, stories told,
Of wipeouts that elicit sighs.

Children giggle, sand sticks tight,
Their castles lean, like dainty dreams.
While mom yells out, "Don't throw that kite!"
The wind just laughs, it seems to scheme.

At sunset, beach balls take their flight,
As laughter blends with ocean's tune.
The day wraps up, a sheer delight,
Until tomorrow, with the moon!

Crescendo at Dawn's First Light

Waves tumble in a morning cheer,
As coffee brews with salty air.
Seashells gossip, crystal clear,
They gossip loud, they just don't care.

The sun peeks up, a golden blob,
While surfers chase a sleepy tide.
They bob and weave, like funny jobs,
And splash like fish, while dreams collide.

A dog runs past, a furry blur,
With sand in paws and joy galore.
He leaps, he rolls, a sandy fur
Masterpiece that keeps us wanting more.

As morning glows and laughter swells,
The seagulls join in pure delight.
With every wave, a story tells,
Dawn breaks with giggles, all is right!

Rhythm of the Celestial Waters

The tide waltzes in a splashy show,
While jellyfish dance, soft and bright.
They float like balloons in a circus glow,
Throwing foam confetti, what a sight!

Frogs-on-surfboards leap with glee,
As dolphins giggle overhead.
Each wave just skips with antics free,
And poets wish they could be fed.

The sunset glows like a clown's bright wig,
Mixing colors in a playful tease.
The fishes start a conga gig,
While mermaids laugh beneath the breeze.

Under the stars, the laughter swells,
As nightbirds hum a breezy tune.
Tales of the ocean, who can tell?
In this watery world, we commune!

Strings of the Ocean's Heart

The ocean croons a silly song,
With ukulele waves on the shore.
At low tide, seaweed plays along,
Tickling toes, they beg for more.

Seashells toss in a crazy band,
Playing beats that make us sway.
A crab conducting with a grand hand,
Commands the surf, come out to play!

Mermaids giggle, flippers flash,
As starfish strut in funky rows.
The coral reef joins in with a splash,
In harmony, where laughter flows.

With twilight fading, we clap our hands,
To every wave, our hearts entwined.
In this concert made of strands,
The ocean sings, our souls aligned!

Ocean's Whispered Melodies

The sea snickers as it rolls,
Tickling shores with frothy holes.
Crabs tap dance on sandy stage,
While gulls squawk their witty rage.

Waves pose like they're in a show,
Making sure everyone gets a glow.
Seashells gossip as they shine,
Who needs a rhythm when waves entwine?

Jellyfish wave with no care,
Hitching rides through water's fair.
The surf is where the fun's at,
A splash here, a flip, and a chat!

So laugh along with every swell,
Each bubble bursts a giggly spell.
The ocean hums a cheeky tune,
Where even fish can't help but swoon!

The Lullaby of Rolling Tides

Waves roll in, a giggling tide,
Whispering secrets that they hide.
A starfish wears a silly grin,
While dolphins play a game to win.

The moon's a joker, tosses light,
As plankton dances, oh what a sight!
Seashells chuckle, "What's that sound?"
The ocean's laughter swirls around.

Crabs in tuxedos strut with pride,
While seaweed swings, it can't abide.
They tap the beat, they sway and spin,
Under water's joyful din.

With each wave that plays its part,
The sea beats out a happy heart.
So let the currents laugh and play,
As tides draw near, then sweep away!

Echoes Beneath the Surface

Bubbles rise with secrets untold,
Whales sing tunes both brave and bold.
Fish tell jokes in colorful hues,
While eels slip through with flippered cues.

Coral reefs chuckle, look at me,
This fish has sprouted a crown, you see?
Octopus crack jokes with eight-armed flair,
While sea cucumbers giggle, unaware.

Drifting seaweed waves hello,
As turtles waddle, nice and slow.
The ocean floor, a stage of mirth,
Each creature laughs, it's truly worth!

Echoes under bubble-filled skies,
The laughter bursts, you can't deny.
With every ripple, joy's confess,
The deep blue is a jokester's nest!

Dance of the Celestial Currents

Stars twinkle as the waves start to prance,
Moonbeams join the frolic, what a chance!
Fish wiggle in their sparkly attire,
Making waves with each flirty choir.

Currents glide like they're on a spree,
Creating whirlpools full of glee.
Jellyfish float, a colorful sight,
In this watery carnival of light.

A sea otter balances a shell,
While her friends cheer, "You dance so well!"
Barnacles hum, "Let's join the fun!"
The ocean's party has just begun.

So swirl with joy, let laughter lead,
Through currents ripe with splashing seed.
Every wave a giggle, every splash a cheer,
In this dance, we have nothing to fear!

Ballad of the Tidal Embrace

When sea foam dances with a flip,
The little fish plot their next trip.
A crab in a tux, oh what a sight,
Claws waving freely, what a delight.

Jellyfish float with an elegant flair,
Wondering why humans swim with despair.
Seagulls squawk jokes from the pier,
While starfish giggle, full of cheer.

Each splash brings laughter, oh what fun,
Mermaids cracking jokes under the sun.
So grab your float, don't be shy,
Join the party as the waves fly high.

With every swell, there's a tease,
As sea turtles spin, oh so at ease.
The ocean's a stage, don't miss your cue,
And remember to laugh, it's good for you!

Crescendo of the Wind-Swept Waves

The breeze tickles noses, what a jest,
As sandcastles crumble, never at rest.
A surfer slips on his own board,
The waves erupt, laughter's reward.

Kites in the sky dance wild and free,
While I trip over my own two feet.
Seashells whisper secrets to the sand,
And crabs hold a contest, you understand?

With every surge, a comic play,
The tide's going rogue, in its own way.
Splashing kids with ice cream cones,
And fish steal fries while we moan.

As the laughter rolls like a wave,
We cherish the moments that we save.
So come join the fun, the tide's our muse,
In this playful dance, you just can't lose!

Overture of the Coastal Breeze

The winds waltz in, with a silly grin,
Tickling the toes, let the fun begin.
A dolphin's leap, a graceful fall,
While kids toss beach balls, laughing for all.

Sand specks fly as the beach train roars,
Squeaky toys echo from shores to stores.
Seagulls steal fries – what's on their minds?
With crinkled bills, they chase the finds.

A sand dune's a throne, all hail the king,
While flip-flops are lost in a funky fling.
Shells make a band, let's join the tune,
With laughter and sizzle, beneath the moon.

Softly the tide rolls in for a hug,
Each wave tells stories, snug as a bug.
So giggle with glee, let your heart seize,
In the coastal waltz with the playful breeze!

The Soundtrack of Endless Horizons

The horizon hums a quirky tune,
While surfers play and sing to the moon.
Octopuses clap with their eight-arm flair,
Crabs breakdance, without a care.

Sandy toes lead a conga line,
As waves keep the rhythm, feeling divine.
Seagull soloists take the stage,
Cawing out laughs, it's all the rage.

A picnic's planned, oh what a spread,
With sandwiches that dance, it's said!
Seashell trumpets join in the fun,
With every wink from the gleaming sun.

So let the waves swirl in a jest,
With sandy laughter, we're truly blessed.
In the echo of the coast, let's sing,
For every wave's a funny thing!

Lavender Hues of Sunset Tides

The sun descends with a peachy grin,
Seagulls squawk like they own the din.
Flip-flops flying as kids lose their shoes,
The waves are laughing, spreading sea-salt blues.

Buckets of sand, castles tall but weak,
Crabs doing the cha-cha, a comical streak.
Splashing about with a clumsy dance,
The ocean's rhythm gives everyone a chance.

Balloons float away, tethered to dreams,
A kite swoops low, or so it seems.
Parents rolling their eyes at the scene,
While kids chase the tide, wild and serene.

As the colors blend and the laughter stays,
We'll chase these moments in silly ways.
With lavender hues painting the floor,
The fun of the tide brings us back for more.

Undercurrents of Timeless Currents

Lost socks bobbing in the swell,
Laughter echoing, ringing like a bell.
Fish in bow ties swim by for a joke,
While starfish attempt to do the stroke.

Sandwiches flying, a picnic gone wrong,
Ketchup squirt mishaps make for a song.
With ice cream drips on noses and hands,
The ocean claps, amused by our stands.

Seashells whisper secrets, oh what a tale,
Of a crab with a pail who's bound to derail.
While dolphins leap in synchronized fun,
With a splash and a dash, they outshine the sun.

A lighthouse winks with a bulb in delight,
As we frolic beneath its custodian light.
The tides keep rolling, and so does our cheer,
In the dance of the waves, we find our frontier.

Ocean's Embrace: A Serene Journey

Once upon a wave, where laughter's the guide,
A rubber duck races with the ebbing tide.
Shouting for mermaids, we search with intent,
But it's just a lost pirate—oh, what a scent!

The tides are a riddle, a puzzle, a play,
As flip-flops float off, in the most comic way.
Sandy sandwiches with a side of surprise,
Eating seaweed salad, just to be wise.

Kids plotting schemes with nets in the air,
"Let's catch a wave," they say with a flair!
The octopus giggles, his eight arms in tow,
Dancing through foam, stealing the show.

As sun goes down, just a twinkle remains,
With giggles and memories, we'll surf the next rains.
The ocean's embrace, quite slippery and fun,
Leaves us craving more, ready for the run.

Painting with the Colors of the Deep

With brushes of laughter, we splash and we play,
The sea paints our feet as we dance in a fray.
Fish in sunglasses swim by with a smirk,
While jellyfish jiggle—what a quirky perk!

Canvas of chaos, the tide against toes,
As seaweed wigs dance in the wind that blows.
Buckets of giggles spill over the shore,
Painting memories that we can't help but adore.

The horizon's our palette, the clouds our brush,
Each wave brings a giggle, a colorful rush.
Parents, like lifeguards, with sunscreen and flair,
While boogie boards wobble through salty sea air.

At last, we retreat, with treasures in hand,
Seashells and stories from this joyful land.
With colors of laughter, we close out the day,
In the watercolor dreams, all worries drift away.

Verses Written by the Wind

The breeze is strumming on a lute,
While seagulls dance in silly poot.
A crab is clapping, oh so loud,
As jellyfish float, all unbowed.

The sun is winking, waves reply,
With splashes that just make us cry.
A dolphin wears a funny hat,
And chortles like an old tomcat.

The sandcastles begin to sway,
As toddlers laugh and misplay.
A beach ball bounces, hits a tree,
And all the fish just laugh with glee.

So cheers to fun beneath the sky,
Where waves and giggles never die.
We'll dance along, so full of grace,
In this ridiculous, joyous place.

The Chant of Briny Depths

In the salty deep, where mermaids jest,
They wear their shells, they're quite well-dressed.
A clam sings softly, trying to impress,
But its off-key note causes quite the mess.

Octopuses with eight arms, oh so spry,
Play hide and seek with each passing bye.
Their ink cloud bursts like a comedic show,
While fishy friends spill beans, casting a glow.

The seaweed sways like a silly dance,
As starfish giggle, quite in a trance.
A swordfish sharpens its wit with delight,
While crabs debate if it's day or night.

Bubbles giggle, floating like balloons,
Underneath the light of silly moons.
Every splash and wiggle brings cheer,
In this briny land of fun we hold dear.

Cascading Notes of the Sea

The waves roll in with a slosh and giggle,
As surfers tumble and do the wiggle.
A sea lion barks, it's a funny sound,
As it rolls and frolics, joy abounds.

Seashells chime in mismatched tones,
While clownfish tease with silly loans.
Anemones poke out their wiggly arms,
Tickling them all with their quirky charms.

The tide rises with a joyful hiccup,
As towels fly like a wild pickup.
Pelicans swoop with a goofy grace,
Diving for fish, a slapstick race.

So let's surf through this chorus of fun,
Where laughter and waves blend as one.
Join the frolic, the splash, the spree,
In this hilarious play of the sea!

Twilight Harmonies at Water's Edge

As twilight paints the sky in pink,
Frogs croak softly, and fish just wink.
A raccoon stumbles, tripping a bit,
While ducks quack loudly, not giving a split.

The water glistens, like a funhouse mirror,
Reflecting giggles that come in clearer.
An otter slides down with a splooshy cheer,
Making all the onlookers burst into leer.

Fireflies dance, making sparkly trails,
As night creeps in with tug-boat gales.
Each splash and ripple creates a joke,
As the crickets chirp, their laughter evokes.

So gather 'round where the silliness flows,
And let the twilight's playful mood grow.
With waves serenading the fun up ahead,
We'll laugh till the stars paint dreams in our bed.

A Canvas of Tides and Dreams

The sea paints with foamy strokes,
Fish wearing hats, they tell jokes.
Seagulls giggle as they take flight,
Chasing crabs that scurry out of sight.

With every splash, the waves do dance,
They swirl and twirl in a silly prance.
A beach ball's fate is up for grabs,
As it dodges the laughter from playful crabs.

Children splash in a watery race,
Mud pies made with goofy grace.
The tide brings treasures, socks and shells,
Each one with its own funny tales.

At sunset's glow, the fun's not done,
Even the whales join in on the run.
Tides sort the hunters from the viewed,
A canvas of laughter, joy renewed.

Serenading Shores at Twilight

The moon whispers secrets to the waves,
As sea turtles practice their cool rave.
Seashells play tunes that make you sway,
While crabs put on a cabaret.

A dolphin slips on a slippery floor,
Makes the crowd laugh with a belly roar.
Waves crash like drums on the sandy street,
As beach umbrellas dance on their feet.

The fish throw a party, all in disguise,
Wearing sunglasses and funny ties.
They flip and flop in a joyful jest,
Singing sea shanties, doing their best.

At twilight, the shores hum with cheer,
Even a crab plays the tambourine here.
The sun bows down, with a wink and a wink,
In this seaside show, all laugh and think.

Sway of the Ocean's Heartstrings

A jellyfish waltzes, so light on its toes,
While a starfish dreams of being a rose.
The waves tease each other with playful kicks,
While seagulls deliver their funny tricks.

An octopus tangoes, legs in a spin,
Leaving all the other fish laughing within.
The coral reefs hum a silly tune,
While clams play peek-a-boo, just like a loon.

Surfboards parade like ducks in a line,
Each trying to show off the best of their shine.
Waves swirl and giggle, a foamy ballet,
Nature's own jesters, having their say.

At sunset, the sea glows with laughter's embrace,
As the tides rock gently, a whimsical space.
Each splash a reminder of joy in the fray,
In this watery world where silliness stays.

Horizons of Harmony in the Blue

In the distance, where sky meets the sea,
A fish in a bowtie shimmies with glee.
The tides have a chuckle, rolling their eyes,
At the seaweed's dance, in a humorous guise.

The horizon winks, as clouds puff with pride,
While shrimp do the cha-cha, they can't hide.
Surfing on waves, a crab takes the lead,
Its moves so quirky, a comical breed.

The ocean sings songs that make you grin,
Shells play the guitar, inviting you in.
As the sun kisses water, they share a laugh,
Even the plankton have a quirky staff.

In this lovely world, where giggles abound,
Harmony bubbles in giggles profound.
Each wave a note in the grand ocean's cheer,
A symphony of joy, always near.

The Infinite Song of the Horizon

On the beach, a crab plays clarinet,
His tiny legs dance, a silly duet.
Seagulls laugh, they try to compete,
But their squawks are less than sweet.

The sandcastles all wear silly hats,
Guarded by crabs and their funny spats.
A wave crashes, knocking them down,
The crabs just dance, they don't wear a frown.

Balloons float by with a funny squeak,
Caught in a breeze, they make us peek.
They twist and turn, what a sight to see,
Just like the fish that play hide-and-seek.

So let's laugh along with the splashy mess,
For nature's jokes are what we confess.
With each swell, there's a giggle and grin,
As tides bring fun, let the laughter begin!

Wavesong: The Ballad of the Deep

Down below, fish sing in a choir,
Their gills sway like they're caught in a fire.
The octopus conducts with a funny flair,
Eight arms waving, without a care.

A dolphin leaps with a comic twist,
Turning flips that you can't resist.
While starfish watch with a puzzled stare,
"Can we join in? We have time to spare!"

Crabs do the cha-cha on the sea floor,
With bubbles rising, they beg for an encore.
"More rhythm, please!" the sea turtles cheer,
As laughter bubbles up, drawing near.

So here's to the tunes in the ocean's embrace,
With funny beats that quicken our pace.
Each wave rolls in like a jolly old friend,
In the ballad of deep, where hors d'oeuvres don't end!

Whispers of the Ocean Tide

The tide dances close, with a skip and a slide,
Whispers of laughter, as seaweed takes pride.
Clams snap their shells, keeping time with the beat,
While little fishes boogie, twirling their feet.

Seashells gossip like old friends at tea,
Sharing tales of waves and occasional spree.
"Did you see the whale? He slipped and he fell!"
Echoes of giggles in a bubbly shell.

The surfers arrive, they're trying to glide,
But tumble and flop as they take a wild ride.
The seagulls all cackle, wings flapping with glee,
"Not so graceful, are we?" they squawk with esprit.

So next time you visit the alluring shore,
Join in the jest, let your laughter roar.
The ocean whispers secrets, funny and bright,
In its rhythmic embrace, it's pure delight!

Melodies of the Rolling Surf

The surf rolls in, a merry old friend,
Combing the beach like a non-stop blend.
Sandpipers dash with their silly fast feet,
Fleeing the waves, oh, what a treat!

Seashells blush beneath the sun's gaze,
"Look at us shine!" in the warm sunny blaze.
With each splash, the waves chuckle and grin,
Bringing joy with the motion akin.

Starfish lounge on the sun-bleached mat,
Complaining of tan lines, how about that?
The crabs perform in their shell-tastic show,
While sea cucumbers just sway to and fro.

So dance with the tides, make music anew,
For laughter and whimsy are just for you.
In this rolling surf, where silliness thrives,
Join in the fun; it's where joy derives!

Lullabies of the Deep Blue

In the ocean, fish have dreams,
With fins that dance in moonlit beams.
A crab plays drums on a shell so fine,
While seaweed sways, sipping brine.

A starfish sings with a turtleneck tune,
An octopus juggles beneath the moon.
The seahorse twirls, quite a sight to see,
While dolphins laugh, 'Hey, look at me!'

The jellyfish wobbles with flair and jest,
Each wave a giggle, life is a fest.
A clam cracks jokes, it's truly quite grand,
As sardines form a well-coordinated band.

With bubbles bursting in bubbly glee,
The deep blue lullabies sing to the sea.
Through waves that shimmer with laughter bright,
Sleep tight, dear fish, till morning light.

Rhythm of the Murmuring Waters

Down by the brook, frogs frolic and leap,
Their croaking chorus, a tune most deep.
The fish flash smiles as they swim with glee,
While turtles float, sipping herbal tea.

A beaver taps out a beat with a stick,
While otters slide down, doing tricks so slick.
The current giggles, swirling around,
A playful party; joy knows no bound.

The crickets chirp in a synchronized hum,
While the water striders skate, oh what fun!
Each ripple dances, a lively parade,
In this joyful world, all worries fade.

So let the waters whisper their song,
In the rhythm of play, where all belong.
Nature's band plays, each note a delight,
Under the sun and the shimmering light.

Echoes Beneath the Salted Sky

Under the sky, where seagulls squawk,
A fishy opera begins with a talk.
With a splash, the seals take the stage,
While barnacles gossip, turning the page.

A whale tells tales with a booming voice,
And crabs join in, they have no choice.
The sardines shimmy, their scales shining bright,
Even the plankton joins in the fight!

As waves uproar, the coastline claps,
With sandcastle hopes that never collapse.
The horizon laughs like it's in on a joke,
Echoing joy till the sun starts to poke.

So let the ocean sing with delight,
With salty rhythms that take flight.
In laughter and splashes, the world feels right,
Where echoes beneath the salted sky ignite.

Harmonies of the Breaking Surf

Waves tumble over with a bubbly shout,
The shoreline chuckles, no room for doubt.
A shell yells out, 'I'm a star of the show!',
As crabs dance around in a sandy tableau.

The sea foam giggles, tickling toes,
With surfboards gliding, how the laughter flows.
Each wave a chorus, singing with cheer,
While dolphins dive in, 'We're here, we're here!'

A pelican pondered, 'What's the best snack?'
As the fish swim by, they launch an attack.
The beach ball rolls off, with a giggle it bounces,
While kids splash about in their goofy pounces.

In the vibrant surf, where merriment swells,
The harmony rings of the ocean's good spells.
So laugh with the tide and ride every curve,
In the melodious dance of the breaking surf.

Songs from the Coral's Depth

Bubbles pop, fish dancing kinda odd,
A lobster spins, now that's quite a fraud!
A clam tried to sing, but it just made noise,
The octopus chuckles, he's one of the boys.

The seaweed sways with a twist and a twirl,
While starfish giggle, it's quite the swirl.
They form a band with a jellyfish song,
But nobody's listening, they all got it wrong.

Crabs start a conga, they scuttle on sand,
The seashells are laughing, they can't understand.
A dolphin joins in, does a flip and a dive,
And everyone joins, hoping to survive!

So grab your snorkel, let's dance in the tide,
Join this wild ocean, it's quite the ride!
In coral caverns, the laughter won't stop,
With scales and tails making jiggles non-stop.

Driftwood Diaries in Euphony

A piece of driftwood, it tells a tall tale,
Of fish wearing hats, in a grand old gale.
With every wave, he sways side to side,
Pretending he's surfing, on a wild, silly ride.

Oh, the tales that he tells, of ships lost at sea,
A captain named Pete, who was scared of a bee!
He scribbles his notes on the sand with a stick,
But his messages read like an old party trick!

The seagulls all gather, they squawk and they shout,
As driftwood makes up stories, without a doubt.
"Pirates and treasure!" they say with a cheer,
As the sunset gives way to the onset of beer.

So raise a toast to the wood, let it sway,
For those with a sense of humor, you might just stay.
An ocean of laughter, throughout the great bay,
With driftwood diaries, you'll be laughing all day.

The Waltz of the Water's Edge

The waves do a jig, a playful charade,
As seagulls dip low, in their feathered parade.
A crab sets the beat, with a clap of his claws,
And all of the fish flutter fins with applause.

Turtles in tuxedos, waltzing around,
With a hint of a shimmy, they glide without sound.
A porpoise jumps high, oh what a sight!
He corkscrews and flips, in the pale moonlight.

The sea cucumber groans, he can't keep the pace,
But the shrimp keep on twirling, with joy on their face.
Anemones laugh as they sway to the beat,
In the rhythm of waves, things can't be discreet!

"Just another waltz!" they all sing with glee,
As currents spin dancers in watery spree.
So sway with the tide, let your worries disperse,
In the waltz of the edge, the verses rehearse.

Liquid Echoes in a Quiet Bay

In a bay so still, with whispers of glee,
The fish all play tag, it's a sight to see!
A snail sings a tune, a slow serenade,
While barnacles jam on the rocks, undismayed.

The sharks throw a party, but keep it discreet,
With bubbles and laughter, they dance on their feet.
The stingrays glide by, doing spins in the sun,
While the turtles chuckle, 'Oh, isn't this fun?'

Pelicans dive down, trying to catch their snacks,
With a splash and a flurry, they cover their tracks.
"Oh fishy fish friends, this is one for the books!"
As the sea becomes laughter, with all of its hooks.

So hear the sweet echoes of joy in the bay,
Where the ocean sings back, in a humorous way.
With a splash and a giggle, it's time to unwind,
In these liquid echoes, silly fun you shall find.

Harmony in the Sea's Embrace

Seashells dance in the tide's sway,
A crab wears a hat made of hay.
The fish have a party, they flip and dive,
While a starfish tries hard to high-five!

Seagulls squawk with a comic flair,
Waving their wings in the salty air.
A dolphin does cartwheels, quite the sight,
While a whale hums a tune, out of spite!

The waves clap hands as they break on shore,
Splashing on humans, oh! What's in store?
A seal does a jig on a rock by the bay,
Laughing at sailors, what jesters they play!

A sunburnt hotdog floats by with glee,
Yelling, "Help me, I'm stuck at sea!"
With laughter and joy, the ocean's in sync,
Nature's own joke, enough to make you think!

Rhythm of the Deep Blue

The waves break like drums, loud and bold,
With fish in tuxedos, all glitzy and gold.
A lobster recounts a terrible date,
While barnacles giggle at the fish's fate!

Turtles glide by in grand parade,
While a jellyfish wears a veil homemade.
Octopi juggle, their humor on point,
As the kelp sways wildly at this silly joint!

Anemones dance, their colors so bright,
While crabs in the corner argue and fight.
Coconuts float as if they are kings,
Proclaiming the ocean's fault in all things!

With laughter and chaos, the tide rolls along,
While fish sing their tunes, off-key yet strong.
The ocean's a theater, each wave a scene,
In this watery world, we laugh and we dream!

Chords of the Cresting Surf

A wave rolls up with a splash and a cheer,
A dolphin stands up, balancing beer!
A clam drops its pearl, oh, what a blunder,
While shrimp throw confetti like they've struck thunder!

Seahorses trot in their fanciest shoes,
While a whale sings ballads, while sipping its booze.
The anchor's a dancer, all rusty and free,
Throwing a party for fishes to see!

The tide tickles toes on the warm sandy beach,
Where a crab tries to dance, no grace in its reach.
With a wave and a splash, they call it a night,
Bidding farewell till the next dawn's light.

With giggles and splashes, the sea carries on,
Turning each mischief into a song.
In this watery wonder, let laughter flow,
Where the chords of the surf steal the show!

Serenade of the Salted Breeze

The breeze tickles noses, with laughter it plays,
Where crabs strut their stuff in the sun's golden rays.
A pelican's dive is a clumsy delight,
Splashing all fish that are giving a fright!

A conch shell complains, so tired of the sound,
While sandcastles topple, the tides are unbound.
Seagulls do ballet, with feathers in fluff,
A show full of antics; oh my, what a tough!

The tide rolls like laughter, a rhythmic parade,
While mermaids sing tunes in a funky charade.
With boisterous joy, the sea holds its breath,
Laughing together, 'til all of them're bereft!

As the sun sets low and the shadows grow long,
The giggles of ocean turn into a song.
Serenading the shore with a wink and a tease,
The salty sea breeze brings everyone ease!

Nature's Crescendo in Solitude

In the garden, gnomes dance wild,
With the breeze, they're laughing, styled.
Worms in tuxedos, having tea,
Chirping crickets join with glee.

The daisies sway with silly grace,
Painting smiles upon their face.
Bees in bow ties hum a tune,
While butterflies gossip at noon.

The Ocean's Lullaby to the Swaying Trees

Trees are twirling, trying to groove,
With waves that wiggle, they can't help but move.
Seagulls throw shade with a cheeky caw,
As crabs on the sand do the cha-cha, raw!

Seashells are drumming on the shore,
Clams and clowns, who could ask for more?
Each splash and giggle, waves get bold,
Nature's fun stories waiting to unfold.

Mare Nostrum: The Heart of the Sea

Fish in fashion, flaunt their scales,
Nautical nymphs sail without fails.
Jellyfish jiggle in pastel hues,
Casting laughter like pirate crews.

Octopus chefs prepare a feast,
With a wink and a wave, not a least.
The anchors teeter, they just can't wait,
As crabs pull pranks, it's quite the fate!

Whispered Secrets in the Surf

Whispers ride on playful waves,
Where secrets shimmer in watery caves.
Starfish giggle, keeping score,
As sea cucumbers snicker galore.

As shells gossip under rounding foam,
Dolphins dance, making the sea their home.
Each splash a punchline, wet with cheer,
As ocean jokes echo far and near.

Ebb and Flow: Nature's Rhapsody

The ocean goes up, the ocean goes down,
A dance of the tides, in a watery gown.
Seagulls are laughing, the crabs do their jig,
While fish are composing a dance quite big!

Splashing and swirling, what chaos delight!
A mermaid is bobbing while avoiding a bite.
The waves play the violin, so playful and free,
While dolphins do cartwheels, just wait and you'll see!

The sun drops its rays, the moon gives a cheer,
I think I just saw a fish shed a tear.
But it's just the salt—no need for alarm,
The ocean's just tickled by its own charms!

So hum to the rhythm, let giggles unfurl,
Nature's the maestro, come join in the whirl.
Embrace all the splash and the joyful yodel,
For every wave's tale is a laugh that's untold!

Tides that Sing to the Moon

The moon winks down with a glimmering gleam,
The waves chime in like a bubbly steam.
Whales are the tenors, starfish keep time,
As squids pen the lyrics; it's quite the climb!

A crab with a top hat starts leading the band,
While fish strum guitars with a quick, cheeky hand.
The jellyfish glow in a swing and sway,
Their twinkling dance sends the seaweed away!

The tides break into laughter, an aqua ballet,
Seashells sing harmonies—who knew they'd play?
With bubbles for trumpets, and foam as our crowd,
It's a underwater concert—let's sing out loud!

So if you hear giggles above the waves' roar,
It's just the sea's humor, who could ask for more?
Join in the fun; here's your cue to sway,
In the tides that sing, the night's here to stay!

The Ocean's Soft Serenade

On soft sandy shores, the ocean whispers low,
As barnacles croon, and the waves steal the show.
A clam snaps its shell, keeping rhythm and beat,
While gulls squawk their notes, aren't they quite sweet?

The surf makes a splash, with humor galore,
Tickling toes with each teasing rapport.
Sheepishly grinning, a sea sponge joins in,
With jellyfish bouncing, they dance on a whim!

Tide pools hold secrets of laughter and glee,
A starfish is blushing—oh, what could it be?
An octopus winks, with a wink and a swirl,
While the sea turtles glide like it's all a twirl!

So if ever you wander where waters delight,
Remember the giggles that spark in the night.
Nature's soft serenade is both cozy and fun,
Join in with the rhythm—let's splash 'til we're done!

Watercolor Whispers in Motion

A canvas of blue, splashed with hints of green,
Where waves tell their stories, a whimsical scene.
The fish wear bright hats, each one a delight,
While crabs roll their eyes, oh, what a sight!

Brush strokes of laughter on foamy white caps,
Some seals are painting with sassy mishaps.
The mermaids are doodling with shells and with sand,
While little fish giggle, a cheeky band!

The sky's a wild palette, with clouds that adore,
Watercolors mingle as they dance on the shore.
Pint-sized dolphins join as they leap with grace,
Making splashes of joy in a breezy embrace!

So wander with whimsy along ocean's shore,
Where every soft whisper invites a encore.
Fun's in the waves, where colors collide,
In this world of wonder, let laughter be your guide!

The Tidal Waltz

The beach ball bounces with glee,
While seagulls dance in a messy spree.
Kids laugh as they splash about,
Chasing waves, oh what a rout!

As the tide pulls back with a sigh,
Flip-flops fly, oh my, oh my!
Sandcastles crumble, dreams afloat,
"Hey! Watch the moat!"—yells a silly goat.

Waves roll in, then out, just like that,
Surfboards and laughter, all in a chat.
With each swell, a goofy grin,
Oh, the ocean's wild, let's dive right in!

So dance, dear friends, on soft, wet sand,
Join the tides, come take my hand.
We'll trip and tumble, a watery chase,
In this tidal waltz, let's embrace the space!

Crescendo of the Crashing Surf

Belly flops and splashes galore,
The waves crash loud, we all want more.
With each swell, we lose our might,
Floating away puts up a fight!

"Look! A dolphin!" a kid squeals bright,
As it leaps, just out of sight.
But wait—was that Mom in the waves?
Oops, it's just Dad, who misbehaves!

A big wave sneaks up, we scream in fear,
Yet all we do is laugh and cheer.
The shore is a stage, the sun our light,
For silly antics, oh what a sight!

In this playful surf, we'll ride the foam,
Creating chaos, it's our home.
With every crash, joy takes the lead,
In the ocean's song, we all succeed!

Melodic Murmurs of the Shore

The seashells sing a funny tune,
As little crabs dance under the moon.
Waves whisper secrets to wandering feet,
"Step right here, find a fishy treat!"

Laughter bubbles at the water's edge,
Sand in our shoes, a funny pledge.
"Wet socks!" we yell as we whirl around,
Oops, the tide's here, it won't be drowned!

Gulls take flight, making a fuss,
Why do they squawk? Just to discuss!
With each tide's rhythm, the laughs resound,
In the ocean's arms, pure joy's found!

So gather your friends, don't be shy,
Dip your toes, let laughter fly.
With every wave, a giggly sigh,
The shore's our stage, oh my, oh my!

Fluid Crescendos of Nature

A beach ball zooms with joyful zest,
Bouncing high, it's quite the guest.
An ocean breeze brings a funny hat,
Who wore it? Was it the dog or the cat?

Tide pools bubble, full of surprise,
A crab waves back, oh how it tries!
"Can you do this?" someone boldly shouts,
As they wobble and dance while everyone doubts.

The sun dips low, painting the scene,
And folks still tumble, even unseen.
Each wave a rhythm, each splash a cheer,
In the dance of the sea, we've naught but fear!

Join the fun, in laughter we trust,
With salty air and sand, it's a must.
Together we'll sing, with pure delight,
In nature's wonder, everything's right!

Seaside Tempest of Solitude

There once was a crab with a hat,
Who danced on the beach with a cat.
The waves rolled on in,
While seagulls wore grins,
Making jokes that fell flat, just like that.

A fish with a dream took a dive,
To join in the fun, he did strive.
But tripped on a shell,
And shouted quite well,
"I thought I could crawl, not just thrive!"

A clam with a knack for a tune,
Tried singing a song to the moon.
But the tide pulled him near,
And oh dear, oh dear,
His lyrics were lost to a swoon.

With laughter, the beach came alive,
As starfishes jived, oh they thrive!
So if you feel blue,
Just join in the crew,
Where oddities gather and strive.

The Sound of Water Kissing Shore

A snail tried to surf on a wave,
But forgot how to balance, the knave.
He tumbled and rolled,
While laughing, we told:
"Maybe next time, just be a cave!"

A gull made a terrible joke,
About fish who had dreams of a cloak.
But they flopped on the sand,
In a band, oh so grand,
While we chuckled and choked on our smoke.

Then a dolphin began to ballet,
Leaping high in a most funny way.
The crowd burst in cheers,
Through laughter and tears,
As the tide led the night to dismay.

With the waves and the crabs in a twist,
We joined in a watery tryst.
From giggles to sighs,
Under starry skies,
We embraced what seemed too hard to resist.

Rippling Harmonies in Liquid Time

A fish with a trumpet did play,
While jellyfish swayed in dismay.
They bobbed up and down,
In a rhythmic frown,
As the shrimp formed a band to display.

A sea urchin, quite shy, took the mic,
With a voice that could spark a good hike.
But it wobbled, then fell,
In a slippery spell,
Leaving crabs feeling slightly less hype.

Then, echoing loud from afar,
Came a whale with a glow-in-the-dark star.
He sang of the night,
What a curious sight,
While the turtles planned dances bizarre.

Thus the waters continued to sway,
With jokes that just brightened the day.
In this wondrous ballet,
We laughed all the way,
Living life in a rib-tickling play.

Dune Dances Under a Starlit Sky

Beneath the wide stars, they pranced,
A raccoon who had always been chanced.
He shook like a tree,
Full of glee, can you see?
While the moon grinned, in laughter, entranced.

Then a crab with a sandwich so grand,
Spilled jelly all over the sand.
The gulls held their breath,
Prompting snickers of death,
As they schemed on a great breakfast plan.

A sea turtle, all dressed in a scarf,
Told jokes that would make big fishes laugh.
But a wave rolled him back,
Into slippery crack,
Where he pondered his own silly path.

With friendship, they danced through the night,
In a festival filled with pure delight.
As the wind played a tune,
To the stars, they croon,
Turning solitude's frown into light.

www.ingramcontent.com/pod-product-compliance
Lightning Source LLC
Chambersburg PA
CBHW072128070526
44585CB00016B/1579